Watch Your Time

Watch Your Time

An Interfaith Spiritual And Psychological Journey

REV. JAMES R. SQUIRE

ISBN-13: 9781540854414
ISBN-10: 1540854418
Library of Congress Control Number: 2016920345
CreateSpace Independent Publishing Platform
North Charleston, South Carolina

We shall not cease from exploration
And the end of all our exploring
Will be to arrive where we started
And know the place for the first time.

T. S. Eliot   "The Four Quartets"

Watch Your Time
Personal Core Values
Interpersonal Core Values
Grit

J. R. Squire   "The Four Quartets" of Our Spiritual and
Psychological Journey

Reviews for *Watch Your Time*

This book is awesome! Reverend Squire has provided inspirational dinner conversation in our household for many years as our 3 children learned under him at EA. They loved to bring home "Revs" lessons and still reference them today. Now he has compiled some of his lessons in this book and shares his four part structure to guide us to the good life with meaningfulness and purpose. This is a book for all ages with a unique perspective of wisdom and adolescent energy that is inspiring.

Jay Wright
Head Basketball Coach of the Villanova NCAA National Championship Basketball Team

Over 38 years, the Rev. Jim Squire was a beloved chaplain and counselor at the Episcopal Academy in Suburban Philadelphia. Over those years, Rev. Squire provided love and guidance to hundreds and hundreds of families - including ours. In this book, "the Rev" (as he is known) shares the wisdom he has gained through the years and asks each of us to be intentional about how we invest our most precious resource - our time and to align its use with our most sacred values. We read: "Consider how different and great your life would be if you realized that redeeming as much of your time as possible to give purpose and meaning to you and others is the true measure of success. Your life could be a series of moments that bring true joy to you and others." Jim continues to spend his time well, in capturing a snapshot of his wisdom and making it accessible to all.

Marie McCormick, PhD
Partner
Insyte Partners

What a wonderful read! What a superb book! Grab this book off your shelf any time. Read it for its clarity, its wisdom, and most of all to remind you that there's something more to life. Jim Squire or "The Rev" lives the lessons he shares. I know. He's touched the life of every member of my family.

Thomas Donaldson
The Mark O. Winkelman Endowed Professor of Business Ethics
at the Wharton School, University of Pennsylvania.

With exceptional clarity and depth, this slim volume puts forth the essential truth that how we spend our time is the key to transforming our lives. In order to live a life of purpose, meaning, passion and joy, James Squire understands, from experiential teaching of an ethics course for 38 years at the Episcopal Academy, that it is not what we have but what we do for others that gives our life value and substance. We will be remembered for a life well lived by losing our lives in order to find our lives. *Watch Your Time* should be an essential read for those interested in the psycho dynamics of the human spirit and by schools, colleges, seminaries, churches, and religious institutions.

Richardson T. Merriman
Chairman and Chief Executive Officer
Pennsylvania Trust

Watch Your Time brings into perspective what's important in life, no matter your spiritual landscape. Reverend Squire presents the material in such a way that each reader can tailor the message to his or her specific relationships, life experiences, and cultural background. His depth of experience and immense understanding of human nature are evident in his thoughtful writing. The text teaches you not only how to watch your time, but how to make the most of it, appreciate the people around you, and live a fulfilled and rewarding life. It is the kind of book you want all your loved ones to read after reading it yourself.

Christy Brevard
Former Student and Class Day Speaker at Harvard's Graduation

Watch Your Time can help everybody utilize their time and navigate relationships with joy, fulfillment, and passion. Through a combination of gripping narrative and interactive exercises, Rev. James Squire gives you the tools to unlock a more meaningful and purpose filled life. *Watch Your Time* is a fast and fun way to make a positive impact on your daily routine today!

Kristin Tate Wood
Investigative Journalist, Social Media Personality and Author of *Government Gone Wild*

For Vicki

Acknowledgment

I HAVE WRITTEN THE following analysis and process from part of an ethics course I taught to bright, engaging students for thirty-eight years at the Upper School of the Episcopal Academy in Newtown Square, Pennsylvania.

These ideas came as a result of teaching that course and learning from my students, both inside and outside the classroom, what really generates happiness, meaning, and purpose in life.

I am grateful to the parents who strongly urged me to get my thoughts down so that others may benefit from the process that will be described in the following pages.

I did not realize how much I used the expression "Watch Your Time" until a group of students reminded me of this.

My wife, Vicki Squire, has been helpful in giving feedback to me and in her steadfast assistance in bringing these ideas to a wider audience. My children, Thaddeus, Adam, and Spencer, and their spouses, Meredith and Courtney, were gracious when I ran ideas by them. More importantly, they have lived out what I have written about in this slim volume. I am grateful to Drew Mason who is always present in the good times and the bad times as a source of support and inspiration.

As you will discover in this book, my four-year-old daughter, Joanna, died of a rare form of leukemia. She was diagnosed on Good Friday and died on the following Christmas Eve. She went through the rigors of a bone-marrow transplant in between those times that did nothing to stop her disease. She died a month or so after we brought her home from the hospital following the transplant. That event informs the importance of time for me, because she had so little time. I am an early riser, but I have a ritual that I set my alarm for eight o'clock even if I have a late commitment the night before or during vacation time. Watching my time, I do that so that I will not waste a portion of the day ahead.

There are times in our life when we need someone on our side who sticks with us in getting something done. Those persons for me have been Richardson Merriman and Lloyd Pakradooni, who wanted to make sure that these ideas got out into the public domain.

My thoughts have been made clearer by my editing team at Create Space.

There may be times where a thought I share may have come from another source, but it has been difficult for me to make attributions, as I have written this small book as a stream of consciousness to capture the information in its purest form. If I have failed to give proper credit where credit is due, I would be grateful for any attributions readers may direct to me.

The Reverend James R. Squire

Introduction

$\mathcal{T}$HE CENTRAL GOAL **of this book is to suggest a method to live your life with purpose, meaning, and joy. We don't think of the obvious. Time defines life. How we use our time defines living. The interaction among (1) watching our time, (2) core personal values (3) core interpersonal values, and (4) grit are the four parts we will consider as essential for living the good life. You are about to embark on an important journey like no other. It will be uniquely yours.**

Overview and Research as Direct Experience with Young People
As I have indicated, the following is what I have learned about happiness, purpose, and meaning after teaching ethics to students for thirty-eight years, as well as from life's good and bad times. The students have helped me enormously to discover what I have learned and have indicated to me that my design for living has helped them (students are the harshest critics). I hope these reflections will be of some help to you as well.

This series of thoughts is meant to not simply be read, but to be experienced. In other words, there is work to be done as you move through the following pages.

One of the things I learned while teaching young people is that we do not remember books that concentrate solely on the reading of words. We tend to "chunk" material that goes to our brain and is remembered.

It is the same reason telephone numbers are not presented as a series of ten numbers—we would never remember them. Hence we learn them as groups of numbers beginning with the area code. That is the way our mind works, and it is important to remember this as you make your way through this guide. The emphasis here is reading small chunks of material and connecting it to an emotion. This allows the material to be more readily accessed when we need to use that critical combination of watching our time, identifying core personal and interpersonal values, and integrating grit into our lives. Those four areas are what we "chunk" with our brain to produce meaning, happiness, and purpose.

The research I have done involves working directly with people. I have been around them in an intense fashion for thirty-eight years and have learned much from them. The research is experiential in nature— of observation and direct experience—not a result of studies using questionnaires or being one step removed from the process. This book is based on real-life exchanges with the world's toughest critics as my research assistants. Teenagers will not tolerate anything that does not work in real time for them. They refuse to be manipulated in any way to believe a certain set of ideas. They question everything. This makes them ideal research assistants.

Research on the brain indicates that a teenager's higher-level executive-functioning skills have not totally developed. My experience, however, is that while executive function of the mind is not fully developed, teenagers have overly developed the ability to read situations they are in and to take reflection and attach it to feelings that, in turn, inform their actions. They possess this attribute because belonging to a group and having good self-esteem are important to them. They, like adults, will do anything to avoid feelings of guilt, rejection, or vulnerability. To achieve these goals, they come to know that they need to watch their time.

My experience is that although the higher-level critical-thinking skills of teenagers may be incompletely developed, their decision-making ability and their grit tend to be more developed. They must over-develop the attachment of feelings to thoughts to compensate for the reduced executive function of the mind. We can learn a great deal from them. Life is a two-edged sword. Teenagers may seem unfocused on the management of their actions (although I do not agree, based on my experience with them), but they may indeed make the best therapists in the world. They can spot a phony a mile away and can read another's behavior very quickly, because they need to, as self-esteem and a sense of belonging are critical to them. Obviously these two important needs of young people are key goals for them.

Teenagers feel deeply! I saw a T-shirt that indicates the direction we need to go as we connect memory and feeling. It read: "Think with the senses. Feel with the mind. Art (of the good life) in the present tense."

We can learn from teenagers that feelings must be attached to thoughts before they are integrated into what we do. Just as we take the critical importance of time for granted, we have taken for granted that perhaps the most important things in life can be learned from those going through adolescence. Our collective cultural context is that adults know best. If something is important, we defer to what adults value. My experience is different. We have a culture that expects little regarding insight from a teenager. We have missed an opportunity to see how the four-part system that we will explore can be seen in young people. They have strong feelings that can be attached to strong ideas and insights. They rise to the occasion. Meaning, purpose, and happiness, long regarded as foreign to any self-respecting teen, can be seen when they finally put together the importance of the interplay of time, personal and interpersonal core values, and grit.

A Longitudinal Study

The advantage to teaching ethics to students over thirty-eight years is that I have my own longitudinal study. I hear from students frequently, and when they put it all together and practice the insights we will cover in this book, they find they are happier and find more meaning and purpose in life. In fact, it can happen to them right away. The issues we will explore can become a rock in the stormy nature of life now and in the future.

Ingredients of the Good Life: Meaning, Purpose, and Happiness

Some find this rock in their relationship with God, or in a relationship with others, or in a cause greater than they are that works for the good of many. The common denominator is that all world religions have a version of the Golden Rule: "Do unto others what you would have them do for you." My whole approach described in this small volume is predicated on the importance of doing things for others. The people who live by the Golden Rule are the people we remember. They are the people whose lives we celebrate. We remember and celebrate what people do that is good, not what they possess.

There are certain things that help a person live the good life and be remembered. There is a saying referred to as the "miracle of these empty hands": we only get to keep what we are willing to give away. St. Francis addressed this thought in his famous prayer instructing us "to seek to love and not to be loved, to console and not to be consoled." Harry Stack Sullivan, the founder of the interpersonal theory of psychiatry, was asked what made a person mature. He did not miss a moment when he responded, "It is the ability to put another first." All of this thinking makes for good reflection in creating one's personal and interpersonal core values.

We must remember the importance of interpersonal core values, keeping in mind the words of the existentialist Jean-Paul Sartre that "heaven and hell are the others." We create heaven and hell for others through our core values. Both personal and interpersonal core values make up the horns of the dilemma of getting our life right to allow meaning, purpose, and happiness in. Each of us has the responsibility of knowing that we can make a person's life better or worse by our actions. Nothing could be further from the truth than the childhood saying that "sticks and stones can break my bones, but names will never hurt me." They will, and they do.

A DISCUSSION OF THE FOUR PARTS

The Importance of Watching Your Time (Part One)

I want you to note the title of this book, *Watch Your Time*, for I feel time is the most important part of this four-part paradigm. Time is something that is too often excluded in our considerations of what creates meaning, purpose, and happiness.

When we stop for a moment to think about it, the use of our time is our most important asset leading to the good life.

Our use of time is as essential to our very life as the air we breathe, but too often we take our next breath for granted. Time and air sustain our lives yet are invisible to us. Time is the central thread. Time affects our core values, grit, and how we can center ourselves and live in the now. Time holds it all together. Watching our time is the key to transforming our lives to experience the good life of meaning, purpose, and happiness.

Time permeates our decision-making, which is a reflection of our core personal and interpersonal values. As you are doing those two exercises in this book, think about how time affects your values and therefore your actions.

We have timed and untimed decisions. Sometimes we have to make a decision in a split second. A few years ago, a person waiting for a subway in New York saw a man fall onto the tracks and decided to leap onto the tracks and cover him over so he couldn't lift his head as the subway train ran over both of them. They both survived. This decision had to be made in a split second, as the rescuer could see the subway approaching out of the corner of his eye.

Time is why the decision to text in a car is so dangerous, as some experts believe texting is like closing your eyes for six seconds. Close your eyes for six seconds, and see what it is like to watch your time for that long.

When a good friend of mine retired, I asked him what was the greatest thing that he was experiencing in his new life. He had been a busy and effective professional educator. He simply said, "I now have control over my time to do more of what I want to do, when I want to do it." Time has changed his decision-making pattern, still based in his core personal and interpersonal values.

I have another friend who was recently diagnosed with a rare form of cancer. After meeting with the doctor, his last question was, "How much time do I have?" That question was haunting him from the moment that he stepped into the doctor's office. The doctor's response was a year or two, and that response directly informed how much grit he and his family needed to acquire to make the remaining time as valuable and meaningful as it could possibly be.

Bill Lyon, sports writer for the *Inquirer*, a Philadelphia newspaper, wrote an article recently after he threw the first pitch during a Phillies game. It was "Let's Conquer Alzheimer Disease" night at the ballpark.

Bill is a victim of the disease. When he received his diagnosis, he wanted to crawl up in a corner for the rest of his life. But he chose to "watch his time" on earth while fighting the disease that he calls "Big Al." Where did he learn to express this kind of grit? I would venture to say that no small part of it comes from writing about known and unknown sports heroes over the years and how they persevered. He was always a great advocate for the underdog. Now he is the underdog.

Since I am writing part of this book after the Olympics, one can see how watching your time literally takes on a whole new meaning in every sport. Swimming and track come most quickly to mind.

Life is a paradox and a trade-off as we "watch our time." There is a price to pay. Any time that we are choosing to do one thing, we are also deciding to not do something else. For Olympic athletes, time in training often means that they are not spending time as typical adolescents or adults, where there is more downtime.

Trade-offs are not limited to such extremes as Olympians. What about parents who spend a great many hours in their profession, prohibiting them from spending quality time with their families? Make no mistake about it—quality time can mean quantity of time.

Life is a series of gains and losses—whether it is grief over the death of a friend or loved one, moving to another city for an opportunity, or choosing to enter another school. Often we think that we just miss the person who died, the friends or family we are leaving for another area, or our past colleagues. We focus on the people. When we begin to watch our time in a more focused way, we discover that it is the time with those people that we really miss and often forget. There is the old adage regarding someone who is dying. We never hear them say, "I wish I had spent more time at the office."

As you consider when you used your values, place watching your time into the equation. If one of your core values is family first, what does watching your time really have to say to you about that core value?

Watching your time can also mean to be aware of when time seems to stand still. Psychologists refer to this often as flow; we also know it as being in the groove. As you consider your core personal and interpersonal values, recall the times you used them and you felt at one with everything that was going on around you. There are two simple examples of this phenomenon. Think about when you are watching a sporting event and the tide seems to turn in favor of one team over another. They seem to be in a groove. Everything seems to be going in the right direction.

Another example is when you spend an evening with friends, and you are enjoying yourself while listening to a great concert. Suddenly the time has ended, and you feel that it has rushed by. You can't believe that the event is over. Watch that aspect of time. Know when that occurs for you. Attempt to get more and more of those experiences into your life.

Try to avoid or improve on those occasions where time drags as though you are crawling through a desert. You may be taking a class where you feel it must certainly be almost over, but just a short amount of time has passed by.

The Importance of Having Our Ingredients for Happiness Become Second Nature

Like a great athlete, actor, or musician, for example, these ingredients of core personal and interpersonal values, watching your time, and grit need to become second nature. That is an important issue. Once these three parts woven together with time become second nature to you, you will enjoy more purpose, happiness, and meaning. The move necessary for an athlete to complete a shot, an actor to remember a line, or a musician to sing or play a song is always right there ready to be used by them. That is the overall goal for these exercises! That is why watching your time becomes the bedrock to help you to live the good life.

Time considerations must be the base of the pyramid, particularly since the importance of time has been overlooked for so long. The most natural thing that we have—our time—doesn't come naturally to us in a heightened awareness of it. It is assumed and taken for granted until it is threatened by something such as a serious illness. We simply drift through it.

Arriving Where I Started as if It Were the First Time

Now let me take you back to when I started to have the idea about use of time. I was in graduate school at Duke and counseling patients in the hospital wards at the medical center. The people with whom I met were diverse: of different origins, race, education, acuity of disease, and faith.

In that setting I noticed that black women patients, on the whole, coped with their illnesses better than other people I counseled. It took me some time to determine why this was the case. My observations resulted in a comprehensive paper titled "The Existential (live in the now) Notion of Intentional Time in Black Women."

Like so many things in life, I have misplaced the document, but I remember my exchanges with these patients as though they were yesterday. Over the years, however, I forgot where I started with this idea as I made my way through life. Black women communicated joy because there seemed to be no tomorrow or yesterday. They focused on the here and now in our exchanges, and you could feel their presence in relationships with them, more than with others. Being present is key!

After many years of teaching young people, the idea of how to live with happiness, purpose, and meaning resurfaced for me. I actually did not see this revelation coming until a group of students told me how I always said "watch your time" when our meeting was getting close to ending, so that they would not be late to their next class. Lateness communicates disrespect for others waiting at the next class or meeting. Lateness communicates that what I have been doing is much more important than what you are doing.

"Watching your time" is key to living life with purpose, happiness, and meaning, along with the identification of your core personal values, core interpersonal values, and grit.

Young people live in the now. It is often said that young people are irresponsible and fail to see the consequences of their actions because of the diminished executive function of the brain I referred to earlier. That is certainly a negative spin on the issue. There may be another way of viewing the failure to see consequences: perhaps it is because they are so centered on the now.

Many things are valued as examples of success in our culture, most often money or fame. But the one thing that is limited and different for all is how much time we have to spend on this earth. Time is our most valued commodity. It has the most value, but it is more often than not taken for granted and forgotten. You learn this quickly when there is a death of a friend or family member, or when you spend any time in a critical-care unit. My daughter, Joanna, died of leukemia when she was four, so this value of time and how we use it has been enmeshed in my life each day that I live.

The fourfold process presented below will be a map for moving through life is, by design, simple and easily remembered, but at times it is difficult to act on. It also assumes that our basic needs are being met—such as food and shelter—but time is the great equalizer. The homeless person and the board chair have the same time constraints regarding death, as we will all eventually die. The old adage holds true that "you can't take it with you."

Time can, however, be more accessible to those in need than those who seem to have everything the culture offers up as success. The cultural definition of success can "trick" people to believe they have everything they need, so that the importance of time is not noticed. This leads many to get what they want but not what they really need. They then throw their hands up and cry out, "What's the purpose of it all then?" If you have a serious health issue or need basic services, you become aware of how important it is to use your time as your most valued commodity.

The importance of time is directly linked to no time left, or death. There is a story about a difficult parent who met with the head of Eton, the fine England prep school. She was disappointed about her son's performance at every level. She raised question after question with the theme of "What exactly have you been preparing him for?" The headmaster's response, after giving her ample time to express her anger, was "death." What the Headmaster was underlining was that the student really needed to use his time well. His time was limited. It was his most important commodity. He had to be better about watching his time.

How we live life is so often shaped by how we view death. I am not talking about the "eat, drink, and be merry, because you may die tomorrow" mentality as much as saying that our time should be focused on purpose, meaning, and happiness.

How our time is spent should be found in how we find meaning, purpose, and happiness. Ultimately, as the research suggests, particularly in positive psychology, that means doing things for others first and having an experience that assists us in transforming the self, such having as a relationship with God, supporting a worthy cause, or becoming a member of a team.

Watching your time is central to the work found in mindfulness studies. Mindfulness underscores the importance of using our time. The tenets of mindfulness are meditation and deep breathing; the goal is being truly present with ourselves and others. This process helps us focus on the now and the ultimate currency of our greatest asset, which is how we will use our time between birth and death. There has been much written on this aspect of watching your time. In essence you focus on your breathing as you breathe in and out. The challenge is to keep thoughts of the past or future out of your consciousness.

Like so many important skills, mindfulness takes practice until breathing and time focused on the now become second nature to us.

Mindfulness is becoming a cultural phenomenon. Various professional schools are requiring it to be taught and experienced, as focusing on the now brings great rewards in paying attention to any task. I would recommend you go to the Internet and choose a mindfulness app or framework for discussion that works for you.

The wonderful thing about mindfulness is that, with practice, it becomes second nature. Focus on breathing in and out, and stay in the moment. It is that simple or complicated! Like anything important, practice makes perfect! Your mind may wander when you begin this exercise, but you will find yourself benefitting from staying more and more in the now. The present moment is all we really have! Mindfulness underscores our central theme that we should watch our time.

Years ago, I remember seeing a book title regarding how kids spend their time. It was *Where Did You Go? Out. What Did You Do? Nothing.* The book points to the need in our task-oriented culture to take a time-out and just be. Usually a "time-out" with friends, with family, or alone can be an enriching experience as well. Watching your time takes on new meaning when we think to ourselves, "Where did all that time go? Time flies when you are having fun."

Perhaps this ability to get to the place of meaning, purpose, and happiness for black women finds its foundation in culture. There are stories of Saturday nights when black people who were slaves would gather in their living space to sing, dance, be with one another, and laugh out loud. It was a raucous, happy time. The slave owner looked out the windows of his manse on the hill and wondered how his slaves could be so happy. Some of the slave owners would actually make their way down to the homes of the slaves and look in the window to see the slaves' secret. What they saw was relief from the grind of their lives and people being truly present for one another, exuding a remarkable presence with one another. What they did at that moment mattered. Thoughts of field, whip, and injustice were relegated to another part of the heart and mind.

The slaves carried no regrets to the dance floor. They did not focus on the pain of the past day or week. Instead they watched their time, focusing on the now so they could transform their lives. This was not a denial of their struggle but an affirmation that there was one place where they could be free and live in the moment. This was powerful because it contrasted with the time in the fields where time seemed to move as a person crawling through the desert on all fours.

All of this four-part process to achieve happiness and meaning is like a mobile. It is a delicate balance among your core personal values, interpersonal values, how you watch your time, and grit.

Consider how different and great your life would be if you realized that redeeming as much of your time as possible to give purpose and meaning to you and others is the true measure of success. Your life could be a series of moments that bring true joy to you and others. It is more valuable than any amount of money or prestige, and it can make a real difference for the better in our world.

Again, the important point is that we are remembered for what we do for others and not for what we have. Think of anyone whom you regard as great. They are people who have structured their time such that their use of time is seen as their ultimate currency.

Those who achieve the purpose of living life with meaning and happiness create positive memories for others. The most powerful positive memories are those that are done with no strings attached where you have nothing to gain yourself. These actions can change the way a person feels—perhaps from despair to hope, from being overwhelmed to being back in control, from the "black dog" of depression to a sense of well-being and others. No one forgets how another person made him or her feel.

In my life's work, I was allocated funds to give to others who were in crisis. These funds were not to be returned, although a good many people did, because they wanted others to benefit as they had. The amounts given were not large, but they were the right amount of money to turn a situation from despair to hope. Words are not adequate to describe the feelings associated with those exchanges. It was living out that wonderful statement about empty hands, "We only get to keep what we are willing to give away." Putting others ahead of our own self is the very definition of a mature spirit.

Think as well of when you have waited for a diagnosis and news of a loved one in a critical-care waiting room. You are intently watching your time, focused on the moment when word will come your way. Whether that is good or bad news, you will never forget how you felt in that moment.

Watch your time! Practice mindfulness, as "the now" is all we really have!

The Analogy of the Four-Part Structure

Here is the image I want you to consider as we begin this journey. We will use the analogy of my favorite beverage, iced tea. The basic ingredient is water, to which you add the tea bag and perhaps some lemon and sugar.

The basic notion of watching your time is analogous to the water. It is the essential ingredient that leads to purpose, meaning, and happiness. Time is your currency. We will put your core personal values into the basic ingredient, similar to the tea bag. We will also add your core interpersonal values to the mix, similar to the lemon. We will stir it using the spoon of grit. Now we will see how these four things come together to assist you in living the good life. This will be our four-part approach.

The Intersection of the Core Personal and Interpersonal Values Is a Powerful Place for Decision-Making

The intersection of our core personal values and core interpersonal values is where our decision-making occurs. Sometimes we have time to decide, and sometimes we do not. Our goal here is to enable your decision-making to become second nature. This results in you making the best choice for you and for others to bring meaning, happiness, and purpose to your life and assist others in finding theirs. Having things become second nature is the fundamental reason that athletes practice for competition, or actors for their roles. I want you to have easy access to sound decision-making. Understanding what makes you tick goes a long way toward giving you more control over your actions.

The Nature of Values

As you are considering your list of your core personal values, the following may be important to keep in mind.

Remember that values are the steering wheel of the soul. Values direct our actions and shape our personal code. The code often contains values that we feel are universal and always true, such as "all people are created equal" or "it is our solemn duty to help rather than hurt."

Values may be a list of attributes such as sound judgment, moderation, justice, or courage.

Religious thinkers might add faith, hope, and love to this list. Almost all religions in the world have stated values. In the West, we are most familiar with the values of Jews, Christians, and Muslims. There are several sources for the values of these three religious groups. They are referred to as "Peoples of the Book," as all three base their authority for action in the written word. For the Jewish person, it is Hebrew literature (Old Testament). For the Christian, it is Christian literature (New Testament). Christians base authority in both Hebrew and Christian literature in the Bible. Muslims consider the Koran the basis for their values.

A key point to remember is that the values of the religions referred to as the "Peoples of the Book" depend on how the sacred literature is interpreted. You may have people who adhere strictly to the meaning of the words now and others who may base the meaning of the words in some historical context, such as what the words meant when they were written. How the word is interpreted can yield different courses of behavior and ethical action.

The traditions of each of these groups that grow out of the word add another layer of complexity to religious values. There are also liberal interpretations and conservative interpretations of any book that represents authority for a group.

Honesty, compassion, forgiveness, repentance, and gratitude are other examples of values. A value can be universal, found in many different cultures. The Golden Rule, to treat others the way that we wish to be treated, is a universal value.

Values can be expressed as a duty where one does something because of a commitment. The most obvious example here is a soldier's duty to his or her country.

More often than not, values are not recorded. Yet everyone knows the rules. The values can be overt so that they are known by all through the verbal or written word. Values can also be covert, meaning the values are unspoken, but what can or cannot be done is known and understood to all. Often the covert values will trump those that are overt.

As you will see below, values can be seen as the reason that you get up in the morning or your reason for living.

Let's begin.

Discovering Your Core Personal Value (Part Two)

I will take you through a simple exercise. I have modified this exercise from "Twenty Things You Love to Do" in the book *Values Clarification: A Handbook of Practical Strategies for Teachers and Students* by Sidney B. Simon, Leland W. Howe, and Howard Kirschenbaum (pages 30–33). I have reduced the number of choices required for the student to make and have added that a feeling must be attached to the final choice. I have also made some other changes that seemed to work better for supporting the new paradigm I am presenting.

Try to do this exercise as quickly as possible so that you are free-associating in making your choices. This will bring about more self-honesty. Do each assignment before moving on to the next step of the exercise. We have been told that your first choice on a true-or-false test is likely to be the right one. This is an example of this process of free association.

The first step is to choose and record ten ideas, issues, or things that you feel provide meaning, purpose, and happiness in your life. Choose things that make you excited to get into the day. These things could be what you feel to be your reasons for living. They should be the first things that enter your mind. Then thoughtfully read through your list, reflecting more on your choices.

Look at all ten ideas, issues, or things you have written down. Watch your time so that you are focused on each item by thinking of examples of each. Think of times when you used each item. Spend a bit of time with this so that you are living "in the moment" with each of them. You are there, reexperiencing the idea, as if it were your first time. It is important that you connect a feeling to each idea. Record these feelings beside each item on the list.

Next, take your pencil and choose five core personal values that you could live without, and draw a solid line through your choices such that you can still see the ideas, issues, or things you are giving up.

Read through the five that are left, taking some time to reflect on each as you did in step 1.

Now choose three of the remaining ideas, issues, or things you could live without, and put a dotted line through those choices. This should be more difficult to do, as you may want to hang on to some of them.

There are two things left. You must choose to let one go, so that there will be only one item left. Place a wavy line through that item and reflect on why you let that one go. Consider your choice and associate a feeling with it. Record that feeling.

Circle the remaining item. Reflect on its meaning and importance to you. Reflect on how that choice affects your decision-making. You may feel this item does not affect your decision-making. Consider to yourself why this is. Sometimes we develop a reference point for deciding not to do something. For example, if your parents appeared as the final circled item, perhaps you say to yourself that you are not going to do what your parents want. They have no power over you. Your parents are still influencing your decision, as you may use them to decide what you don't want to do or be. Doing the opposite of what they want still reflects that your decisions are based on your attitude toward them.

Consider your last circled choice and contemplate ways it affects what you decide to do. Go through the steps of reflecting on examples and attaching a feeling to it. Record the feeling. You are there!

You have now identified your core personal value that is one line (horizontal) on a grid. You have made it real by feeling that you are there watching your time. You have attached the thought or item to a feeling.

The Discovery of Our Interpersonal Core Values (Part Three)

One of the key ingredients overlooked in decision-making that results in watching your time, happiness, and the promotion of meaning is your interpersonal core value. In some way, the world of interpersonal relationships has a direct bearing on how decisions are made that promote happiness and a sense of purpose for the self. More importantly, interpersonal core values have the potential to promote happiness and a sense of purpose in others. This is the transformative nature of what we are deciding while we are watching our time. Every decision creating purpose, happiness, and meaning is tied to our interpersonal values.

When you do the exercise below for the discovery of your core interpersonal values, consider how much watching your time is involved in acting on each value. Take for example the values "we will be present," "we will be on each other's side," and "we will be available to one another." Watching your time needs to be a guiding point for this process. Let me underscore an important issue as you apply watching your time to any of the other three parts mentioned: personal core values, interpersonal core values, and grit. Let's say for example that today you took ten minutes to be "truly present" for another, or you spent thirty minutes with your family to reflect a core personal value of "love of family." Given the spectrum of time over the course of twenty-four hours, this does not seem to be much time given to any of these issues, *but* there is a more important point. It is also about how readily you can access these values over a longer period of time. The critical issue and goal is when you reach for them, they are there. They become second nature.

To begin the process, read through the following descriptions of what happens in a relationship. Take time doing this so that you can reflect on the various topics and think of examples that may apply in your life. Choose three or four of these bold statements to focus your reflection. As you identify your core interpersonal values, these will form the vertical line on your grid.

I refer to the following guidelines in relationships as "Inventing the We'll and Discovering Fire." We often focus on the personal core values as the place that affects decision-making and creates a life of meaning, purpose, and happiness. We forget the power of relationships. I think our interpersonal core values are overlooked in this process, which is why I am going to take a more complete look to see how our decisions are influenced by our relationships. We will see how relationships can be one key part of our four-part approach.

There is white space for your personal comments that will help you in narrowing the field to your key interpersonal core values, as you did with your personal core values. Do not rush through your reading and consideration of these core interpersonal values. Take time to reflect on each one. Some values will produce a distinct feeling in you or bring up an important memory. Use these feelings and memories as a key to ranking your choices and to understanding interpersonal relationships.

I urge you to explore the meaning of each "we'll," as they should be seen as parts of the whole. Each section has meaning on its own but can only be fully understood in terms of the whole series of "we'lls." This process is like holding up a precious stone to the light. You can focus on the beauty of one facet or side of the stone, but the stone only has beauty when it is seen as a whole. Each part is essential, but the whole is greater than the sum of the parts. Certain key ingredients appear in various sections and may seem repetitious. It is my hope, however, that you will approach the reading of these sections like holding a precious stone up to the light and turning it gradually around so that you can see many different perspectives of the same stone. Also in this guide, important aspects of relationships are approached from several different perspectives to enable you to discover the manner in which these perspectives blend to make up the beauty of one person relating to another.

It is a human tendency to want to get things organized into neat divisions and chapters. We enjoy experiencing life as "one thing following another" in a linear fashion. I have purposefully not done that with these sections that follow, for the beauty of the human experience is that we do not experience life in a linear fashion. Life is not a psychology textbook. It is not neat and tidy. Like the precious stone turning before our eyes in the light, we experience life as a whole, with each fragment creating a vital part of the brilliance the stone emits. That is why you may choose one or more interpersonal core values for some may blend together in your thinking like looking at the various facets of a precious stone. I have found this to be the case in my work over the years with students.

The brilliance of the precious stone is perceived by seeing light reflecting from the facets. A stone that is kept in darkness does not have the opportunity to bring beauty to this world. Light needs to reflect from it and to pass through it so that the stone may become aglow with possibilities as we see it "new" with each turn of the stone in our hand.

Your experience in relationships with others is the light that will bring possibilities to see the "new" that is contained in each section of "we'lls."

People in today's world are experiencing tremendous burdens that can be lightened in relationships. These burdens become too heavy at times, causing us to feel broken and alone. We need to have a wheel of a different kind to turn things around. We need to enter into a new contract with one another by committing ourselves in relationships with the words "we will." We need to "invent the we'll." I have included in this small volume some ideas that can help us start to move our personal burdens over the terrain of our existence, so that we can commit ourselves to another cultural revolution that begins with one…with you… with us…by inventing the we'll.

The invention of the wheel is seen as a landmark along our evolutionary trip through the ages. Today we need to invent the we'll—we will work together to achieve significant relationships with one another, and we will be effective and caring in our relationships with others.

The discovery of fire is regarded by humankind as a key cultural advancement. Can you imagine the first people attempting to get fire to work for them after being burned repeatedly in the process? Can you imagine the joy they must have felt when it began to provide warmth and the ability to cook their food? Today people are being burned in a different way in relationships. The pain is emotional and just as intense as physical pain. We need to rediscover the fire of love that reflects in the night sky so that we may hear the words as we gather together in our modern villages—"we will build a better world"—the seeds of which are found when we commit ourselves to another in relationship…friend, student, colleague, or family member, with all that is implied by the words "we will."

I believe everyone wants to be able to love another and to experience being loved by another. There are various levels of achieving this fundamental human need and desire. The purpose of the following words to live by is to help fellow travelers along this life's troubled way to fulfill this fundamental longing. Everyone can find this important jewel of loving and being loved in life. Although we have learned how to speak with one another, some have not learned to converse with others in such a way that we experience a kind of significant bonding and a sense that we will work together in this relationship.

What do I need? What do I want? What do others need? What do others want? What are the characteristics of those relationships that work? What gets in the way?

Life is not something we do only on weekends. We cannot limit our focus to our work life during the week, and then feel that we can spend time on relationships only on the weekends. This kind of thinking makes us part-time people. Think of the following "we'lls" as "bonding bytes" that must permeate all of our lives together. There are no shortcuts to significant encounters, but there are some simple goals that can help us deal with the complex nature of human interaction, mainly putting people first and experiencing excitement and joy in life. These goals will help us get the most quality from the quantity of time that is available to us.

There is always a yearning in us to return to the "good ole days." It is human nature to forget the painful parts of the past as we remember only what was enjoyable. Part of this desire to return is also a desire for us to feel and know again what was important about being young. Hence, a great deal of what I believe about establishing lasting relationships has come from my experience with young people. By entering their world, we can not only learn the issues that are important to them, but we can also see even more clearly what adults yearn to experience as well.

Now begin. Take the precious stone of understanding the nature of relationships in your hand and hold it up to the light of your unique perspective and experience. How will that ever-turning stone look to you?

We will be present. When I was a boy assigned the unwanted task of cutting the grass, I would ask my father to sit outside and watch me cut the grass. I cannot imagine a more boring thing to do, but he would watch me. What I wanted was for him just to be present. He did not have to do a thing. All I needed was for him to be there. But as I look back on the situation today, it was also a way for me to get his undivided attention. One of the ingredients that build solid relationships is giving another our undivided attention. Paying attention to another is not as easy as it seems. Being able to be genuinely interested in another requires some work on our part. Work must be done to empty our own self so that we can fill it with the meaning created in a relationship.

When we are truly present, we are able to enter another's world. The universe is composed of two people, and the music is understanding. People like to feel that someone else is there just for them. We must listen and not be thinking of the next thing we will say when it is our time to talk. People can sense when we feel that our words are more important than their words. We empty ourselves so that we can be filled. We empty ourselves so that we can fill another with the gift of being there.

Being there for another is difficult if we are not there for other aspects of life. We can only focus on another when we take the time to focus on something of beauty that lies around us—a cloud formation, the bright colors of a tree changing, the rich colors of a sunset. Being present for others is a way of life. We spend a great deal of time thinking about the past and contemplating the future, but people respond to those who live in the now. People grow when they are grounded in this moment of time. Living in the now is like a tiller on a ship, for it enables us to steer the moment into the proper direction as we catch the wind. When we are present with another, it is similar to wind, tiller, and sail reaching that point of harmony where we feel at one with what is going on around us. This is different from a desire to possess and to call the other "mine." In fact, the feeling is the opposite of possession, for when we experience that "at oneness" with the other, like the experience with the wind in the sail on the sea, we experience that wonderful sensation of freedom. You are free to be you and free to encourage the other to live in that moment and find important parts of his or her unique spirit.

It is interesting to note that when two people fall in love, this important aspect of being present appears in its clearest form. Whether two people are teenagers or adults, the people who are around them may not understand, for all that the two wish to do is to be with each other.

Part of the work we must do when we are struggling to establish significant relationships with others is to discover those parts of the other that we truly want to be with. We have all felt at one time or another that a friend is that kind of person who we just like being around. Actually, what we are saying is there are important characteristics of the other person that we connect to. What is it about another that attracts us? Can we widen our range of the parts of the other person that we want to be with? People know when we like being with them. It is not something one can fake, since we feel it at those very important places within ourselves that help us discover the authenticity of an experience. Each person is a gift with his or her own unique package. If we approach each individual with that kind of perspective and anticipate that in the unwrapping we will find something that will surprise us with a sense of joy and wonder, just maybe we will expand our sincere feeling that "I want to spend some time with you."

It is a wonderful experience when we sense that a person genuinely enjoys our company. We become more alive when we feel that others want us along with them. This feeling was a valuable part of our experience as young children and perhaps an even more valuable part of our experience when we were teenagers. Remember how you felt when you could finally say to yourself, "I have found a good friend." We long for this feeling again as adults. Whether it is the experience of growing up in a neighborhood, on the street corner, or at a camp, the sounds of those places still speak to us, for they are the sounds that speak to our heart. In our heart we know, given the choice, "They would rather be with me. They choose my company."

We will be on each other's side. When I am in a relationship with another, I need to feel that he or she is on my side. People respond to us when they trust that our actions will be in their best interest. In other words, we want what is best for the other even to the point of putting our own needs second. Someone has suggested that a good definition of maturity is the ability to put the needs of another before our own. We must learn to value ourselves but also be able to put ourselves second to a higher principle: that of the sanctity of the relationship. I have found that the more we put others first, the more they do so for us as well. It becomes a wonderfully energizing positive cycle. But it is all a matter of the intent. Another can sense when you are giving in order to get something back. It will always feel as though there are strings attached. Another perspective is needed, such as, "You only get to keep what you are willing to give away." Giving and receiving are really the opposite sides of the same coin.

It is very energizing to feel that someone is on my side. In the words of the sixties song, someone is there to "stand by me." We stand there as sides are chosen for a game. How good it feels when our name is called. How much I dread being last or next to last to be named. "They want me on their side. We will be together."

A good way to communicate that you are on someone's side is your willingness to inconvenience yourself for the other. This very powerful action produces the feeling that I am with you "through the good times and the bad times." That message touches all of our souls and inspires us to want to respond in kind to the other. "That's what friends are for," as the lyric of the song tells us. We dislike fair-weather friends intensely, for they are the opposite of what we yearn for.

We will be available to one another. It is important to communicate availability to those with whom you wish to build significant relationships. Availability is a state of mind. It is an attitude on our part and an important perception on another's part. To be available to another does not mean that we are always "on call." The other's wish is not your command. Availability means that one should see interruptions in one's day as an opportunity to be an agent of change. Life is not packaged neatly; the real opportunities to be helpful come most frequently when we least expect them to. When we communicate a willingness to make adjustments to be with another, we communicate a strong message about how we value that person. We can make ourselves available to another when we communicate an investment in finding time to meet the other's need. Notice that those who are busiest (in the most creative use of that word) are usually those people whose "door is always open" for you.

We will not major in minor things. We need to be aware of the fact that what is important to me may not be important to another, and vice versa. One of the ways of empowering a relationship is to take seriously what another takes seriously, and to honor those issues that may not seem as important to us. It is equally important, however, that we choose issues that are regarded with mutual importance to be the focus of our communication. Overlooking something that both parties feel is important, while caught in the swamp of the trivial, is unhelpful.

We will recognize the power that is present when two people are in a relationship. We will recognize the political nature of relationships, acknowledging that relationships are concerned with distribution of power. When people think of politics, they immediately think of groups or nations getting their share or trying to determine the nature of the relationship that they will have. The same is true when two people meet. There are three positions that one can take: one up, one down, or equal.

When one begins a relationship with another, there is often an investment in one or the other to be in the one-up position. This automatically puts the other person in a one-down position. When someone is in need of an another person, that someone is usually in a one-down position. This is the position we will experience when we go to a doctor or a teacher for help. They have knowledge or expertise we need. At other times we encounter another who is in the one-up position because he or she becomes the "know-it-all." Contrary to what one would think, people put themselves one up when they feel one down or inferior. It is a very lonely position to be in. People put themselves in a one-down position when they are not confident about their abilities, when they feel that the other has the ability to rescue them from a problem, or when the other holds power or authority over them. Real intimacy occurs when we meet one another on equal ground. When power is shared, we feel in control of our lives. We feel we have the ability to be masters of our destiny.

We will possess the courage to be vulnerable to one another. I like the analogy of life as a card game. As is true in a game of cards, we must play the hand we are dealt. Life may not seem fair, but realizing that helps us to move forward along the way. The hand we have is all that we have, but we must do the best we can with it. Relationships become significant when we risk showing our cards to the one across the table. We usually keep our hand of cards close to our chest, each card representing such feelings as guilt, fear of rejection, and insecurity. We hold them tightly in clenched fists. No one will see. However, the person across from us lays his or her cards on the table for us to see. This is a risk. When it occurs, and we experience that kind of courage in another, we feel free, compelled even, to drop our hand and allow the other to see who we are. Sometimes this is done one card at a time, for everyone is different, and everyone has to have some secrets.

We will realize the grass is not greener on the other side of the fence. We can only grow in a relationship when we come to accept our own sorrows. There is a story about the Tree of Sorrows. Once people die and reach heaven, they are free to walk around the Tree of Sorrows and place their sorrows on the tree. After they place their sorrows on the branches, they must walk around the tree and remove someone else's sorrows from it. Once they circle the tree and see the sorrows of others, they wind up picking their own back off the tree.

We will remember that the only thing we have control over is our own feelings and reactions. Our first inclination in a relationship is often to get control over others by having them change their behavior in a particular way. If we could only get them (or the situation that they have created) to act differently or feel differently toward us, everything would be all right. The old adage that "you can't make someone love you" speaks volumes. However, when we realize that the only thing that we do have control over is our own selves and how we respond, then we have moved forward. We can't change another person or situation, but we can change how we respond to that person or situation. We deceive ourselves into believing that it is easier to change another than it is to change ourselves.

We will live life with a sense of urgency and passion. This becomes the glue in relationships. We have only been given today. For that matter, we have only been given this moment. When people have been confronted with personal tragedy, they tend to "live for the moment." We see this most graphically in a critical-care waiting room. Everyone is intent on hearing the next report from the doctor. Everyone is present for the other. Everyone understands what a passionate commitment to the "now" means. Everyone just understands. Words do not even need to be spoken. A shared experience of intensity becomes a glue that holds those relationships together.

We will assist each other in becoming independent so we can meet the ultimate goal of interdependence. Often we want the person with whom we are relating to be an extension of our own self, to be the way that we think he or she should be. But people resist becoming something that others want them to be. What we yearn for is to be in a relationship with someone who will help us discover who we are and thus achieve independence. When a person achieves independence, that individual is better able to achieve the higher goal of interdependence in a relationship.

The relationship that begins with any form of dependency must move to a relationship of two independent persons becoming interdependent. The job of a parent is to work oneself out of that job. The job of a teacher is to learn to be the best student. The job of one person is to empower others to become truly who they are so that they reach their moment of authenticity. One of the hard lessons of life is that no one, ultimately, can make us happy. Happiness must come from within.

It is interesting to note that the word "pupil" describes a student off to school as well as a part of the eye. It is thought that the origin of this connection between student and a part of the eye originated when a small child sat on the lap of an adult and peered into the relaxed eye of the other, seeing his or her reflection—seeing the reflection of a small child—discovering his or her personal truth. When we look into the eye of another, we want to see our truth. Life is hell when we see ourselves through the eyes of others.

We will remember that emotions are like food. Sometimes those who are hungry for emotional responses from others push those people away by abusive behavior. They yearn for emotional food but push away the very people who could give it to them. The more they need, the more they push away the potential givers of sustenance, to the point that they almost starve. We need to fight through the challenge of their "acting out" so that they truly feel our response and truly feel fed. Suicide is starvation of the soul.

It is known that many people who went through the Depression of the 1930s were without adequate food. Food was on many minds. Later in life many of these same people, after achieving significant financial success, would keep large stockpiles of food in their homes even though reality said, "You will not do without again." Their past deprivation of food was still informing their lives in spite of the trappings of security.

This is also true of our emotional life. Many of us did not get certain emotional food that we needed as young people. We still crave for that emotional food today in whatever form it takes. For most of us, it is to be accepted and loved for all that we are. We need to discover the "starvation" in another and feed that emotional hunger. At times we learn by giving to others what we did not receive as a young child. We have all heard someone say, "I'm not going to be like my parents when I have children. I am going to treat my children differently." This different ingredient is something that people did not get in their younger years at home, and they want to make sure others receive it from them. As Gandhi said, "Even the Lord himself would not stand before a starving child except in the form of food." Within this context we must empower the other to discover his or her own way of developing this much-needed emotional food, as seen in the following words: "Give a man a fish and you feed him for a day; teach him how to fish and you feed him for a lifetime."

We will acknowledge that sometimes we look for emotions or characteristics in another person that we ourselves do not possess. The old adage holds true that "opposites do attract." The outgoing person may seek as a friend or lover someone who is quiet and reserved. The risk-taker may seek out another who is more cautious. What we are attempting to achieve within ourselves is a vital balance or homeostasis. For example, since risk-takers may not have developed a cautious side, they seek someone else in a relationship who will stop them when they have gone too far out on a limb. Likewise, people who are very organized and have every minute of their life planned may choose for a friend or lover someone who is very spontaneous so that they, in turn, can feel a sense of spontaneity and freedom through the attitude and actions of another. We tend to live vicariously at times through the emotions of another.

We will realize that sometimes we enter into relationships that can best be described as a "mutual admiration society." Two people who are very much alike enter into a relationship because they have the same interests and the same style of personality. We quickly realize that they are seeking validation from the other of these similar parts of their personalities. We may hear two young people say with great pride: "You and I are the ultimate party animals." Two other people may look at each other and say: "Isn't it great that we don't feel the need to be competitive with others?" They feed off one another by supporting either the parts of their personality that they want to encourage as ideal or those parts of their personality that they are insecure about and question in their own minds.

We will persevere in the relationship knowing that it is always darkest just before the dawn. Succeeding can be a matter of hanging in there for just seconds more, not always hours. It is a matter of inches, not always miles. One of the significant elements of a relationship that has risen above the ordinary involves not giving up on the other. We may not like the actions of a person, but we must continue to support the person to nurture the relationship.

We will initiate in the relationship. We will care enough to begin. Beginning is the gesture that leads to healing. We have often wanted something from significant others in our life, and often that something—recognition, understanding, love—has been withheld. There is power in the hands of the person who will not give us what we want. There is similar power in not giving to others what they want. We learn that withholding is an act of power. Power produces a sense of security, however false it may be. When we feel threatened in relationships, we fight or flee, and often that fleeing takes the form of withholding what we know the other wants. Initiating takes courage, for we must risk rejection, but it is the only gesture that brings healing.

We will realize that we will do almost anything to avoid the feelings of guilt, rejection, and vulnerability. We spend enormous amounts of energy to filter these emotions out. We struggle to prevent experiencing them at all costs. We rationalize to avoid guilt. We do anything to belong. We attempt to avoid feelings of vulnerability by building structures of permanence. This is most clearly seen in the security that we strive for in the form of success. Since these emotions can dominate our decision-making and actions, we need to be mindful of when they are determining too much of our lives.

We will realize that when we are experiencing emotional pain in relationships, one or both of two issues are present: our self-esteem and our own sense of belonging. Examine your self-esteem or your desire to belong when you are experiencing emotional pain. We all need to feel good about ourselves. We need to be more self-accepting. We all yearn to belong, particularly when our self-esteem is low. I may be inferior, but we are magnificent. The group to which we belong becomes our primary identity as we seek to carry out a shared purpose. We want to belong because it is one of the best emotional investments available. We get so much for our "emotional buck" compared to what we have to give. We yearn to belong to a group that will assist us in achieving either a more moral or immoral purpose. A group that we long to be part of can bring out the best or the worst in us.

We will seek to understand more and to evaluate less. Most significant personal growth occurs in an atmosphere that is free of judgment. It is always helpful to attempt to understand a situation *first* and to assess its ethical ramifications second. When we remove judgment from a situation or exchange, we are free to do things right. But more importantly, we are free to do the right thing. The human impulse is to do good—it is our basic human nature.

We will examine the price we are paying. We are all paying a price in life. What is it? Is it preparing us to love? If not, should we change our course of action? What are the values that are determining the nature of this price? Everyone *is* getting something from a relationship. We are at our best when we attempt to "have no strings attached" when we relate to another.

We will strive to assist one another in achieving greater self-acceptance. We are at our best when we operate from the premise that "thou shalt not have to justify feelings." What we feel is what we feel. Your hair color is your hair color. Your feelings are your feelings. Period. Those feelings (like hair color) should not be up for debate. When we deny a negative feeling or emotion, we give it more power. When we acknowledge the feeling, we can bring it into the light and transform it to a higher good. All evil is good waiting to be transformed. This is the essence of the fairy tale "Beauty and the Beast." The ugly or undesirable can be transformed by embracing the beauty of unconditional love where no strings are attached.

We will realize that another person can be a mirror of our own internal self. Because we want to see ourselves in an "ideal" way that conforms to our own self-image, we are at times prevented from seeing all of the many aspects that make up our inner world. In a very real way, we do not want to know all that we are, for we sense that there are desires and wishes within that we simply do not wish to claim. They are just too repulsive to us to think or feel. However, an emotion or desire left unacknowledged has a power over us. Awareness becomes the key to new understanding.

Let us use an analogy of a film negative. All film negatives have to be developed in order to see the picture. Parts of our own internal self-image are like the film negative. We cannot make out the image until it is developed. This development process lies in the nature of relationships that we have with others—we see the picture when we look at characteristics of another person who we either like or dislike intensely.

One may think, "I can't stand Jane. She is so selfish. She only looks out for herself." Jane may, in fact, be all of those things, but we tend to feel particularly strong about those parts of others that are also parts of ourselves. What that individual recognizes in Jane is probably a strong impulse that the individual has been successfully fighting within himself or herself. Another may say, "George has such a need to control others. I just can't stand that about him." In all likelihood that individual is also saying, "I have great difficulty accepting that part of me that wants to control others." Historically, psychologists have referred to this process as "projection." If we think of the life of someone being a slide that is shown by illumination (awareness) on the screen of another, then indeed this process of seeing our inner life in the lives of others has been aptly named.

As the adage goes, "Do not throw stones in glass houses," or "There but for the grace of God go I." We should be quicker to understand ourselves and others instead of being quick to judge. Judgment does not allow us to see the picture. Understanding does! Picture yourself pointing a finger at another. Then realize that you have three fingers pointing back at you.

This process is also seen in our identification with another. We think some elements of our inner life are good and desirable, but for reasons that are beyond our awareness, we are not able to claim these parts of ourselves. Someone said that "imitation (the process of identification) is the highest form of praise." Recently I saw an interview with a famous talk-show host who had grown up in a blue-collar neighborhood. All of his life, he was taught that what was truly important was done by your hands and the sweat of your brow. The importance of any job was seen in the amount of physical labor you had to put into it. This person loved words. He liked to speak. He liked to make others laugh. Making a living by talking would be the lowest form of work in the community where he grew up, for "talk is cheap." He was only able to claim this important part of himself (the film negative) when he realized that he was imitating, by his actions, the great TV talk-show hosts. He was able to see the picture of this important unclaimed part when he saw how much he identified with those TV personalities and their work.

His development process was one of identification. He finally heard the message that talk can be very important in bringing happiness to others.

When we feel strongly about certain aspects of another person, know that it is saying something very important about part of our own inner world.

We will acknowledge the importance of the role of criticism in our lives. The criticism of us by others can teach us some important lessons about how we truly feel about our own selves. We tend to react defensively with great anger when we secretly believe that criticism by another is describing who we really are. I just completed watching the Summer Olympics. Imagine someone coming up to an Olympic runner and stating: "You're really out of shape and not very motivated, and you have to be one of the slowest people who I have ever seen." The runner—and anyone who overheard this accusation—would probably shake his or her head and wonder what planet this individual making these outrageous comments had been living on. His or her words or criticism would not stick. It would not register, for an Olympic runner is sure of his or her physical prowess and great motivation to be the best.

Now let us take a look at another situation where the criticism sticks. A particular student does extremely well in all of her courses. By everyone's assessment she is a gifted thinker. But this student secretly feels that she has fooled others into believing she is intelligent. She may be saying to herself, "If they only knew how stupid I really am, they would laugh at me." Her internal perception does not conform to her external reality. She receives A after A on tests in all of her courses. Then one day she gets a B on a math test. A classmate makes the offhand criticism, "You're really not so smart after all!" The criticism sticks. It registers, for no amount of external reinforcement of how well she is doing can combat that inner voice of doubt about herself. Ninety-nine people could say to her, "You are the finest student in the school." One could say, "You are not so intelligent." She will believe the one. This criticism hurts and stops her. A change of perspective is needed. She needs help from herself and from others to see that she needs to work just as hard correcting her "inner grading system" as she works in achieving high grades in her courses.

We will realize that people in relationships are like questions and answers for one another. When we enter into relationships with others, we raise certain questions for ourselves and for others, and we provide certain answers for each other about the truth of our own inner life. Questions are raised in our relationships with others. "How much do I trust her?" "Would he continue to be my friend if he knew that…?" "How am I going to tell my child or friend or parent how I really feel about what they have done?" Answers are provided by relationships as well. "I have earned your trust." "I can accept that part of you that you are struggling so hard to accept yourself." "I will risk being vulnerable, for I have to tell someone how I feel." Where question and answer become one is where unconditional love is present. My ability to love you is deepened when I experience your ability to love me.

We will acknowledge a fundamental drive in people: the more we have, the more we want, whether it is matter or emotion. Part of us has a "consumer mentality" toward possessions and people. We want more things, and we have increasingly higher expectations for emotional return in relationships. Our culture has sold us a "soap opera" definition of love based in sentimentality and not in sacrifice. The mature person is someone who can put the needs of others first. This results in the kind of joy that cannot be experienced when we are the primary focus. An example of this phenomenon in action is the parent who receives genuine joy as a result of watching her child open Christmas gifts. No gift could match the joy of watching the surprise and delight of the child. You have to lose your life (sense of self) in order to gain your life (true joy and meaning).

We will strive to operate in reality. We will do this by acknowledging all aspects of our personhood. By recognizing all feelings, we are free to change them or to continue to involve them in our repertoire of life, but acknowledgment or "emotional ownership" of these feelings or parts of ourselves must come first. We all possess an inner ideal of who we think we are. Sometimes this inner ideal does not conform to the feedback others give to us. If this is the case, we become defensive, not allowing the outer picture that others have to touch our image of who we are. The more we get in touch with our true inner self, the better we will be able to assess our role in the world realistically. Does this outer feedback conform to our truth or not? Blaming, denying, rationalizing, and placating are several common ways we attempt to change the outer impression to match the inner perception.

We will recognize that trust is the steel with which the bridge of relationships is built. When adolescents in particular are asked to comment on what they feel is the most important aspect of friendship, they are quick to indicate that trust must be present in the relationship. The same is true for adults. We only share those inner feelings we cherish with another when we "know" they will be treated with ultimate respect and care. This, in turn, allows us to increase our own self-acceptance of all that we are, and growth soon follows. We need to be the "bearers of one and another's secrets." Gossip ruins people and communities. Confidentiality (honoring and respecting the secrets of another) enhances the life of a person or a community.

We will be "actively" empathetic with another. Empathy is a key ingredient in the development of a significant relationship. It is at the heart of outstanding counseling. Empathy is not simply sitting by and wondering what it is like to be in another's situation. Empathy is an activity—an action where we attempt to enter the world of others to feel what it must be like to be them. "What is it like to walk in someone else's shoes?" is the proverbial question that goes to the heart of the matter. Those whose attitude and perspective is one of "help me understand what it is like to be you" are people who possess an essential ingredient for establishing a meaningful relationship.

We will affirm a person's fundamental need to be recognized, to feel needed, to know that he or she is making a difference. Everyone needs to feel recognized, and in a more meaningful sense than Andy Warhol's statement that we all get fifteen minutes of fame. Fame and recognition are very different, yet they are often confused. In fact, those who seek fame and find it often feel empty, since fame reflects more on one's reputation and less on one's character. Those who seek fame are often misled, for what they secretly desire is recognition. Recognition touches the soul of another, since it indicates that we are leading a life with purpose and that this life is a reflection of one's character. We need to know that what we do matters. Part of this recognition will come from those around us, but part must come from within. Self-validation is necessary. We must know that our actions have meaning apart from external feedback, or we will constantly be looking for affirmation from others, making our personal happiness too dependent on the whimsical nature of the world.

One of the ways to receive self-validation is to serve others anonymously. Real fulfillment comes from this kind of action, which in turn nourishes the self and leads to higher self-esteem. But there must be a balance. Self-feedback and feedback from others can be a powerful impetus to produce a cycle of feeling that we are people of purpose. An older gentleman once shared with me his secret of personal success in life. He stated, "Everyone needs a reason for getting up in the morning." He is right.

We will realize that all relationships have an implied contractual nature to them. Rules develop. Certain subjects can be talked about; others cannot. There are expectations. Relationships change, and so must the rules. If change does not occur, the relationship becomes stagnant and oppressive. If rules do not change, conflict occurs because of mixed expectations. Clear contracts assist in the development of clear expectations. Clear expectations assist in turning conflicts in relationships into a creative experience.

We will regard conflict as part of the energy of the relationship. Conflict is inevitable when expectations change more quickly than the contract we have with self or others changes. We expect things of ourselves, and we expect things from others. The most unrealistic and painful expectation is that we will never make mistakes. When expectations are not met with self and others, we become angry, and our anger often leads to conflict. Having expectations for self and others that are clear and reasonable is an important first and often last step to resolving conflict and moving the relationship to a new and better place. Conflict is the energy of creativity and change waiting for direction. It is not to be feared. It is to be honored.

We will acknowledge the fact that life is a two-edged sword. One of the basic principles of life, and in particular of relationships, is that every dimension of a relationship can work for us or against us. However, it is more helpful to see these opposites as one positive charge and one negative charge. It is not helpful to think in terms of categories such as good or bad. Like the battery, when both polar aspects are acknowledged, they can bring power to the relationship. If we deny or repress feelings regarded as negative, these negative feelings will increase in power.

Several examples highlight this point. It is human nature to want to give a little to get a lot. We all participate in an emotional lottery where we put down an "emotional dollar" and expect a "million" in return. Once we realize this, we become more open to the give-and-take of relationships. We must recall the axiom "There is no such thing as a free 'emotional' lunch." It is more important as well to remember that you only get from something or someone what you invest in that experience or person.

There is also the two-edged sword of independence/dependence, compliance/defiance, and responsibility/irresponsibility. People who communicate an extreme independence are guarding against feelings of dependence. Dependency cuts both ways. The dependent "innocent victim" is in a powerful position, for he or she controls so many around him or her. When we are helpless, we are not responsible for our actions. Everyone else is. At the same time, dependency on anything or anyone gives disproportionate power to that substance or person.

People who are so compliant, doing everything we wish them to do, will manifest a defiant part of themselves in some way. Likewise, extremely defiant people have a compliant side they keep secretly hidden from public perception.

Those who are super responsible like to have the relief of being able to be childlike or irresponsible in their behavior. Hence, some of the most driven people will seek a means to allow their irresponsible side to take over.

The key is balance. We see this in the basic elements of fire and water. Fire can burn you or provide heat for survival. Water is essential for life, but too much can flood a home or life and be destructive.

The key balancing agent is experiencing love in the unconditional sense from God or another or from within our own self. As a theologian once said, "When we discover how to love, we will have discovered fire for the second time."

We will come to some understanding of how our intentions and self-fulfilling prophecy are key ingredients for elevating a relationship from the routine to the meaningful. Several studies of teacher/ student relationships have proven that the way in which a teacher views a student can determine the relative success or failure of that student. In one study, a teacher was told that a group of students who had a high ability rating was inferior in intellectual capability. The result was that those students performed significantly below their academic ability. Another teacher was told that a group of students who had an average ability rating was superior in intellectual capability. The result was that those students performed significantly above their stated academic ability. There is a tendency to become who we and others think we are. We tend to do what we and others think we can do.

We will be more intentional in our relationships. Not only do we become what we intend to be, but relationships become what we intend them to be. When I was reading to my then four-year-old son, I often did not remember the content of the story. My intention was to give him the joy of hearing the story. My intention was not necessarily to remember the content.

Relationships are similar to this account of reading to a young child. If we go about the relationship with an intention of just having routine exchanges, largely based in function such as "pass the salt," the relationship will become routine without much grounding in feelings or affection. If, however, we wish to create a relationship with shared mutuality, like when reading to a child, we need to have meaningful follow-up and discussions about the book. This creates true dialogue and genuine shared interest. The relationship will be based on feelings, affection, and involvement. We all have and need "pass the salt" relationships, but they are becoming much more numerous than those characterized by true dialogue and inquiry into what each of us finds meaningful and important.

A relationship will often become exactly what we intend it to be, and we need to be aware of what we want and what our intentions really are. We must realize the difference between intentions and getting what we want. We often intend one thing but get something different and feel that "this is the last thing that I want." If a relationship is not what we want, we must come to terms with what we are receiving from it, for we are all getting something. What part of us is that something filling? What need is it meeting? If you feel a particular way, the person producing that feeling wants you to experience that even when he or she protests to the contrary.

We will take seriously believing in others. Some of the great experiences in life are captured in those moments when someone believes in us when we temporarily fail to believe in ourselves. We do not forget those people. Each of us, if fortunate, has had a person or persons support us unconditionally. That person is someone whom we would do anything for…"swim any ocean." Many times that feeling develops when we realize the other person gave us a chance when no one else would. Another example of experiencing this unconditional support is being surprised by a reaction that we get from another. For example, when we expect to be criticized or judged, we instead receive forgiveness and acceptance. The experience of the other remains with us at a deep level, for we know that the other is interested in understanding first and evaluating second.

We will take seriously our need for intimacy or closeness versus our need for distance or a sense of independence. We see this lesson graphically displayed in the animal world. Porcupines need to huddle during the winter months to keep warm. They need that kind of intimacy for survival. But soon they begin to stick each other inadvertently with their quills, and they must distance themselves from one another in order to survive. Our relationships are similar in that we engage in the ebb and flow of intimacy and distance. Both the warmth of intimacy and the autonomy of realizing our own uniqueness in the world are needed. One without the other would put our emotional survival into question. We can only experience intimacy when we encourage the other to experience his or her individuality. We will be most able to truly experience our individuality, to move to interdependence, when we have a base formed in an intimate relationship. Intimacy is a basis for security from which we empower others.

We will recognize that there are at least three sides to any argument or issue. The sides are yours, mine, and at least a third perspective, "the chemistry of the relationship". This chemistry consists of how our respective attitudes and hidden agendas mix and merge in our communication. Most people now realize that more communication occurs beyond the use of words than we realize; this is referred to as "meta-communication" and is described aptly by Ralph Waldo Emerson's words: "What you are shouts so loudly in my ears that I can't hear what you say."

We will participate in the perspective that life is to be either enjoyed or learned from. This is true for life as a whole and relationships in particular. This is not to say that one cannot learn from joyful experiences. We can, and we do. In fact, part of the dynamics of motivation rests in the fact that we tend to want to repeat those experiences that we are good at and enjoy. However, many have learned the most significant things about life when they have not gotten what they wanted. It seems that the great men and women of past and present have been tested in some significant way by the "hand that has been dealt them."

Hardship and pain force us to strip away superficial references for how we should move forward in life. The hardship and the pain that bring us to our knees force us to find our reference point in the core beliefs, principles, and values that we hold. It is at that moment that we come to an understanding of what F. Scott Fitzgerald meant when he wrote, "There comes a moment in time in each of our lives when we discover who we are, and in this moment, we realize that this is what we have always been and what we will always be."

The same holds true for relationships. All aspects of the relationship should be factored into our enjoying and learning from each other. The hard times we encounter with another, when seen as opportunities to learn and grow, will become important pieces of nourishment for the relationship. A muscle grows and develops by being torn, and then by being given the opportunity to heal. After the healing process, the muscle is stronger than ever. The same is true in relationships between people. However, when we exercise, we are thinking of a three-stage process. We know we will experience some degree of pain for our expended effort. We will allow for healing with a period of rest. We will expect the part of the body exercised to be stronger. When we exercise, we are in control. We or a coach or instructor determine the number of miles to run.

In relationships, we often get caught in the first of the three stages. We fear rejection, guilt, and vulnerability. Anger or personal pain can produce all three. If we will change our perspective when in personal pain or conflict to look for ways to "rest" or bring about healing, then we can see our way through to experience the accompanying personal growth. The Nike advertisement "No pain, no gain" is a truth for life, and within the context of life, it is a truth for our relationships with one another. No one would exercise if it were all pain. Likewise, no one could endure pain in relationships unless he or she could experience significant gain. This period of "rest" is not a period of inactivity or passivity.

"Rest" in this analogy means to seek renewal. The kind of rest we need is to listen to one another with "the third ear." The third ear is that part of us that seeks actively to understand another and to know what it is like to be the other. One of the fundamental yearnings of the human heart in a relationship is to feel that another truly understands what it is like to be us. Rest occurs in the context of understanding and in making sense of what has occurred. The psychologist Bruno Bettelheim indicates that people can tolerate anything that makes sense to them. Finding the "how" in relationships is possible only after we discover the "why." After the "rest" of understanding comes the gain of a relationship based in new and perhaps more reality-based strength to care for one another.

We will realize that our feelings and thoughts are not always known to another person. Because we feel or think strongly about certain matters, we assume the other person must know. Our thoughts and feelings are like a radio within us. If the intensity or volume of the sound increases, we make the mistake of believing that those around us surely must be "hearing" what is going on within us. This fault in relationships is usually accompanied by the words, "But you should have known." Few of us have been given the gift of reading minds. Strong convictions, intense feelings, and important thoughts need to be shared with clarity and directness in order to avoid misunderstanding.

We will realize that those who shout with loud words or actions do not feel heard. Since our thoughts and feelings are like a radio within us, we need to realize that people turn up the volume when they do not feel their "sound" is being heard. Those people speak louder and louder to the point of screaming. Someone can also "speak loudly" by acting out his or her dissatisfaction in not being heard with behavior that causes others to notice him or her. Since this prompts a response, screamers and those who act out feel heard at a superficial level, so they continue to scream or act out. Their own "internal radio" needs to be heard before they reduce the volume of their words or deeds. We must remember that there are two ways to turn a radio down. You can pull the plug, which is similar to rejecting the person, or you can gradually lower the volume, which is similar to attempting to hear what that "inner radio" of the other is really saying.

We will acknowledge that we have an underlying need to possess material things and people. We want to say: "You are mine." There are various reasons for wanting others to be ours. Parents, friends, and lovers want others to be exclusively theirs because they always "know what is best for the other." From our own perspective, we know what has brought meaning and joy to us, and we assume this experience, idea, attitude, or value must be good for others. Often it is, but often it is not. Indeed, the way to hell is paved with good intentions.

For parents, friends, or lovers, the other could be what provides them with meaning, so we wish to have control over that important feeling. "Without her, I am nothing." "Without him, I would be alone." When a spirit of possession is present, strings are attached. "If you really loved me, you would…" "I work so hard so that you can…" "If you really were my friend, you would…" The goal of relationships should be to move from an attitude of "strings attached" to an attitude where "strings are cut." This creates a movement from conditional to unconditional love. Conditional love gets the other "to do" out of fear. Unconditional love gets the other "to do" out of respect. Fear and respect are two primary motivators of behavior. The measure of a person is what that person does when no one is looking. When fear is present, people do the right thing when people are looking. Their goodness is limited to the public domain. When respect is present, people do the right thing when people are looking and when they are not. Their goodness is all-encompassing, existing in both the private and public domain. When respect is present, people continue to do, to be, and to give after they get what they want.

We will acknowledge that our parents, more than any other person or group of people, determine who we are. Parents are the transmitters of values, behavior, and attitude. They become the reference points in all relationships. Even when we say we will not do a thing that our parents want us to do, they still remain the reference point for the opposing behavior. As a result of growing up with our parents, we have an ideal of who we should be and who significant people in our life should be. We are in a constant state of molding ourselves and others to these expectations. These expectations can assist us in setting personal goals. "I am…" "I want to be…" "I need a friend to be like…" "My image of my lover is…" But often these expectations are formed at a time in our life when we were not able to be realistic about them. If the expectation for self or others is not realistic, we may feel: "I just don't measure up," "I'm not good enough," or "He/she isn't quite what I need or want." The ideal self states: "I must be perfect" and "You must be perfect." The real self says: "No one is perfect" and "Our flaws are what unite us." By nurturing us along by guiding us with realistic expectations, parents teach us how to form more loving relationships. What more important role could one have?

We will acknowledge the power of the "familiar" in our lives. We tend to enter into relationships that have an emotional familiarity about them. These relationships generate feelings that make us feel "at home." "At home" is a good expression here, for most of our "feeling environment" was developed in the context of the home, where parents were the key formative factors of our emotional life. If we were raised in an environment where criticism was a common ingredient, we may look for a relationship later in life that contains that element of criticism, even though that critical environment may not be best for us. We choose that emotional environment because it makes us feel at home.

We will claim the importance of friends in our lives, since we all need to belong. Friends are the best relationship investment we have. Whatever you invest in the relationship with a friend, and it can be relatively small, you get so much more in return. This is partly due to the number of friends in your circle. With friends, one part of us wants to possess, but another part wants to include as many as possible.

The power of friendship lies at many levels. Our sense of self or identity is very important to us. At times, we enter into an "emotional deal" with our friends so that our identity can be lost in the identity of the group: "I may be inferior, but we are awesome." If we feel included, then we do not feel excluded or rejected. On the other hand, if we can exclude others from a group, that exclusion will guarantee that we will not be rejected. We will do almost anything to avoid the feeling of rejection. The power of a group of friends is much more than adding up the personal power of the individuals involved. A group of friends can make good-intentioned people better and bad-intentioned people worse. Friends have great power to help and to hurt. Sometimes a group of friends can have their own shared communal values that can set them against society. Not all values are shared, but the core values must be shared to be part of the group. This ultimately sets up a form of opposition. We are this! You are that! This power to help is the basis of support groups such as Alcoholics Anonymous. This power to hurt is the basis of groups such as the KKK.

Friends tend not to talk about the nature of their friendship. This is the power of friendship; it just is. If one friend does a favor for another, usually no big fuss is made. It is just what you do. This dynamic can lead to the phenomenon of being used or taken advantage of. Similar to the relationship with parents, the contract at times can be more open and flexible and perhaps unclear. When a relationship is assumed and not clear, one has to guard actively against abuse of power occurring within it. There is no trust that the other will be with you "through thick and thin." Another issue in an unclear relationship may be the imbalance of power, resulting in being taken advantage of or taking advantage of someone else.

Friends provide us with the important experience of being part of something greater than the self, and when we experience this, we feel personal satisfaction and meaning.

We will acknowledge that in the relationship between two people, a "third person" is present. For example, relationships between lovers are always love triangles. Two people cannot enter into a relationship as lovers without an invisible "third person" overseeing the relationship. That third person, referred to by some as our conscience, comprises all those people who have influenced our values. Our conscience speaks to us constantly as we consider what is right and what is wrong, what we should and should not do. Hollywood depicts the issue by showing someone contemplating doing something wrong with hand on chin. Next, we see the devil appear over one shoulder saying, "Go ahead, do it." An angel quickly appears over the person's other shoulder saying, "No, that's not right. Don't do it." Simplistic as it may seem, that visual image points to a reality in our relationships.

We will acknowledge the fundamental importance of responsibility and balance in our relationships. Responsibility is a direct outgrowth of the importance of respect. When we feel respect for self and others, we also feel accountable to self and others to act in our best interest and in that of others. Best interest will be defined by our values, principles, and personal code of behavior.

Obviously, there will be times when what is best for us will not be best for others, and vice versa. Relationships are a balancing act. The image of a juggler comes to mind. The juggler begins with two or three items and then adds to them, increasing the number of things he juggles until we feel the excitement as we say to ourselves, "How does he do it?"

The number of items brings excitement, but so do the kinds of items. Fire and flashing blades pique our interest and fix our vision on him quicker than balls or bowling pins.

We are like the juggler. The more we become intent on balancing the many items in our life—desire to possess/desire to empower, desire to love/desire to be loved, desire to give/desire to get, strings attached/strings cut, fear/respect, and so on—the more exciting and meaningful our lives will be. The more we become intent on discovering those items that are like the fire and the flashing blade, the more we become aware of the passion that brings the most excitement and meaning to our existence. The more successful we are in balancing the number of items and the adventure of living, the more we will be able to succeed in our relationships with those around us.

Now reflect on your notes in the white spaces.

Do the same thing that you did with the personal core values. Take time to focus on the items above or "We wills" and attach a feeling to each example. What spoke to you about your choices? Think about how your interpersonal and personal core values affect your decision-making. Where they intersect is a powerful place from which you may be making your choices. Once you have an understanding of these values and their role in your life, you can have greater control over how you make decisions.

Now put your core personal and interpersonal values into the central ingredient of how you watch your time. How do these values help you focus on what is happening right now? How do they enrich your life so that you are truly present with others and can focus on something greater than you? How easily do you feel that you can access your values in the day in and day out of life? Do they make a difference in your living the good life?

Even though we live in a culture of relativism where the individual knows what is right without regard to social implications, in our heart of hearts we do know what is right and what is wrong when we see it in our actions or the actions of others.

Do your values help you do the right thing?

Notice where your one core value intersects with your three or four core interpersonal values. That intersection plays an important role in how you decide.

Grit (Part Four)

We will now focus on grit. It is the mixer. Grit is the ability to go on when most people would give up. Grit is seen as one of the key elements to success in life. The old adage holds true that "it is not a matter of how many times you are knocked down as much as how many times you get up." Where does it come from? How do we nourish it?

Grit is based in memory. Sometimes our memories are based in fact. At other times, we remember what adds to our ego ideal or how we want to be seen by others. The proverbial fish story is an example of this. A foot-long fish we caught has increased to two feet in our minds by the time we get home to share the news with others.

Memories are more powerful when we attach feelings to them. Powerful memories are the ones where we overcame something in our past as a result of our perseverance. Such memories produce feelings of warmth and intimacy that we yearn to relive. We are inspired to survive whatever situation we find ourselves in. Those memories give us the power to work against all odds.

There is the frequently used quotation spoken first by the German philosopher Friedrich Nietzsche: "What doesn't kill me only makes me stronger." Memories of when we moved through a challenge by means of personal courage can be used later on to encourage us to face dilemmas that frighten us and to move through them as well. Attach a feeling to that courageous moment in the past that will enable you to access that same kind of courage more quickly when needed again.

There are also memories that can produce a "mantra to move forward." Marketing people know this. Look no further than Nike's slogan of "Just Do It!" My personal favorite guiding mantra is one given to us by Churchill in the midst of his leadership in preventing Hitler and the Germans from conquering Europe and Britain. Churchill's mantra was just three words, "Never Give Up."

Memories that inform and empower can be like food for someone who is starving, for they can nourish us in life-giving ways. Memory plays a key role in world religions. For example, this is true in Judaism during the high feast day of Passover. The Jewish people recall through the foods that are part of the celebration of the holiday that they must never forget the living God who brought them from the bondage of Egypt to the Promised Land. As a Christian clergyman, I experience the power of memory in Christendom with the words offered by Jesus at the Last Supper as he shares a meal with his disciples. Referring to the eating of the bread and the drinking of wine, he says: "Do this in remembrance of me." These words are repeated during the sacraments of Eucharist or Holy Communion and are a powerful part of the liturgy.

It is important to consider what produces grit in people. We get a clue to this by looking at the work of a Holocaust survivor, a climber of Mount Everest, a movie called *Cinderella Man* based on the life of James Braddock, and the content of certain children stories.

Victor Frankl, a survivor of the Holocaust, developed a theory of psychotherapy called logotherapy. When he was asked how he had survived the Holocaust, he focused on several things. At the center of his focus were the memories of his family that he kept alive in his mind. Those memories were a go-to place when he needed sustenance to carry on.

He had a family album of recollections in his mind that he would picture, hoping to experience that kind of love again.

There was also an internationally famous pianist who would practice classical music in his mind and with his fingers while he was interred in a concentration camp. He left the camp far more talented at the keyboard than when he went in.

Beck Weathers survived an ill-fated climb up Mount Everest. Jon Krakauer documented this climb in his book *Into Thin Air*. Weathers has addressed numerous groups and has created a video of the story of the climb. He was on the brink of death, was frostbitten to the point that he would lose some of his extremities, and was operating blindly, lacking food and water.

At the end of his lecture, Beck Weathers makes the point that he is just like the rest of us. "We are all made of the same human clay." We all have the capability of surviving the worst. He emphasizes what he learned from his experience. He indicates that it was just unacceptable to him to never see his wife and children again. The desire to see them fueled his remarkable "miracle" of moving from the brink of death to a new life. It began with him simply opening his eyes on his snow-covered face.

His memory was so powerful that it kept him moving from death to life. He realized that he had traveled the whole world over looking for meaning and purpose, and he discovered on that mountain the realization and memory that meaning, purpose, and happiness were in his own backyard in the form of his family.

Memory produced his grit.

Cinderella Man is a movie that depicts the struggle of James Braddock in his efforts to gain enough money to support his family during the depression. He is a professional fighter who works menial jobs to earn money, but it is not enough, so he returns to the ring to box once again.

The movie depicts brutal moments in Braddock's comeback. Punches land, and the viewer wonders how he can possibly move on. However, with each devastating punch that lands, there is a flashback to his children and his wife. They are memories that can only be described as love and intimacy. His memories are connected to these very strong feelings. He always gets up off the mat and fights on. He has grit based in the memory of his family.

Bruno Bettelheim, psychologist, has written extensively about the power of children's fairy tales to help them cope with the world around them. The one childhood story that comes to mind for me is the very familiar *The Little Engine That Could*. In essence, it is the story of a little train that is called upon to take important cargo over a mountain when most larger trains would not do it. As the little engine struggles over the mountain, we hear the train say that classic line: "I think I can! I think I can!"

When my oldest son was a toddler, we were living on a road that had a steep grade. I would take him out and walk behind him as he was riding his tricycle. When he hit the steepest part of the grade, I saw him rise from the seat and put all of his effort in getting his bike to move forward. There always seemed to be a point where he was struggling for that next burst of energy. He looked like a horse-race jockey having left his seat, trying to propel his horse forward. It was then that I would hear him say: "I think I can! I think I can"—making the words of the little engine that could become part of who he was, forming his grit.

Grit is a universal need. It is something we all respond to. The story of *Rocky*, a Philadelphia legend, became an overnight success because it touched a basic human emotion that all of us yearn to have. Who among us would not be stirred with emotion as Rocky heads up the steps of the Philadelphia Museum of Art to a crescendo of music? Emotions peak as Rocky jumps up and down, arms held high, when he reaches the top. This scene touches us at a feeling level, and that is what makes the difference. Overcoming long odds produces a universal response yielding a gratifying feeling. Deep down inside, we all love a challenge, no matter how small or large it may be. Being "gritty" is celebrated in our culture.

It is often said that "there are no atheists in foxholes." Your foxhole obviously does not require you to go to war. It can be when the bullets of life's overwhelming situations come your way. Prayer is often a go-to place when we have our backs to the wall. Prayer can be made even more accessible in those moments if it is part of our daily practice. Prayer is communication with God. It is a relationship, and like all relationships, it functions best when it is worked on and becomes part of our daily life. When this happens, like the key shot of an athlete or song lyrics for a vocalist, there is access that becomes second nature. It is no different for prayer. If you want to know what is most important to people, just ask them what they want you to pray for when you are with them.

CONCLUDING REMARKS

The Mixer

Now it is time to stir the mix of time, core personal values, and core interpersonal values with the stirring rod of grit. If you don't stir it, you do not get the full flavor. It doesn't blend well. You don't get the taste you are really looking for. What feelings and memories result from the mixture? Taste and feelings go together. You can remember how you feel about places and people just by savoring the mixture. The whole mix is what is important—not just one ingredient. Removing an ingredient changes everything.

We stir this mix with the stick of grit! Grit enables us to get through the hard times. Grit enables us to do what we never thought we could do and is a key ingredient

Watch your time…your core personal values…your core interpersonal values…and grit, the ingredient that stirs the mix, are all needed to develop meaning and purpose in your life.

Before we mix and stir, leading to a life of purpose, meaning, and happiness, we must integrate into our being all four ingredients one at a time, associating each ingredient with a strong feeling.

Doing this exercise may initially feel as though a minute is an hour. Our goal is to be in the moment, watching our time so that our hour will feel like a minute. We want all the ingredients to come together so that they are experienced as one taste. In this case, it will be a taste of the good moral life.

Start watching your time. Think of a time that was filled with purpose, meaning, and happiness, including an example of when you did something for another. Choose a challenging moment so that you can employ memory-building grit. Stay with this moment and focus on it by doing deep breathing, and pay attention to what you are feeling. Consider your personal and interpersonal core values.

Now practice. In order to get this experience to feel as though it is a minute long, you need to practice. But here is the difference with this approach of "watching your time." Feel with your mind and your senses throughout a day. It is difficult to take a time-out during a typical busy day. In the same way that you take a break from work or to eat a meal, take a short period of time even at the busiest of places to renew yourself through this exercise.

If you are someone who enjoys running or working out, I believe that we have an advantage. We have to fit the run or exercise in. When I am running, I find that this is an ideal moment to "watch my time." It's all there…the watching of the time, the feelings associated with a core personal and interpersonal value…and the grit that it takes to push myself a bit further, and the ability to focus on the now. As silly as it sounds, I sometimes find myself saying out loud when I am challenged, "I think I can? I think I can! I think I can." Other times I find the grit by finding a memory that contains the feeling of grit. It often can be of someone else in my life who has exhibited courage and is concerned with others before himself or herself. I have been blessed to have many such people in my life.

The Goal

When considerations of time help us live in the rich moment of now, inform core personal and interpersonal values, and develop grit so that we can more readily access these ingredients, we can increase our meaning, purpose, and happiness.

Watching your time makes all the difference in achieving this goal. It's the central thread. It is so important because its importance has been taken for granted and assumed for so long, much like the air that we breathe. It is ironic that what gives us life and marks our living is air and time. We have time, and we breathe in and out. Those are the two fundamental aspects that define living. Death occurs when we breathe our last and we have reached the end of our time. These two things, time and breathing air, are primordial, which means they are also essential for the propagation of our species. That makes them so vital.

On the other hand, the time that we have to take to breathe is so much a part of our life that, paradoxically, it becomes assumed and forgotten.

We need to reclaim this fundamental truth for us to watch our time as our most valuable commodity. This will inform our legacy and how we will be remembered. Watching our time will breathe new life into us during the good times and the bad times, just as it did for the black women I met on the hospital ward at Duke Medical Center and for those slaves who transcended their circumstances on a dance floor during the worst times in slavery.

Watching our time needs to be at the center of our experience.

About the Author

THE REVEREND JAMES R. Squire has spent thirty-eight years teaching ethics as the head chaplain at the Episcopal Academy near Philadelphia, Pennsylvania. He specializes as well in bioethics, faith development, positive psychology, counseling psychology, diversity work, and the development of student leaders. He was chair of the Religion Department. After the 9/11 attacks, he created a national conference on "Understanding Islam."

Squire has served as chief pastor to thousands of people who make up the school community. He was a founding board member and counselor at the Marianist Counseling Center in Chester, Pennsylvania. He has served on the board of the Middleton Counseling Center in Bryn Mawr, Pennsylvania.

He holds degrees from West Chester University, Berkeley Divinity School at Yale University, and Duke University where he was the Jarvis Traveling Fellow to Duke from Berkeley. He was among the first in his family to attend college and values his work as a laborer in a steel mill to pay for his college education as one of the most valuable learning experiences of his life.

He now works to assist Episcopal schools at the national level in any way that he is needed.